Edition Schott

Alexander Rosenblatt
*1956

Sleeping Beauty
Jazz Fantasy on a Theme by Tchaikovsky

for Piano Duet
für Klavier vierhändig
pour piano à quatre mains

ED 23209
ISMN 979-0-001-20892-5

www.schott-music.com

Mainz · London · Madrid · Paris · New York · Tokyo · Beijing
© 2019 Schott Music GmbH & Co. KG, Mainz · Printed in Germany

Preface

When I decided to write "Sleeping Beauty", I knew that I would only use the theme of the extremely famous waltz from Tchaikovsky's ballet, as did Paul Pabst in his concert paraphrase over a hundred years ago. I brought a new jazz style to the tune while leaving it quite recognizable at the same time. While composing this piano duet, I tried to apply vintage jazz elements (chords, rhythms including swing, melodic lines, etc.) as naturally and intelligently as possible so as not to destroy the original music. I hope this piece will become quite attractive and effective for both performers and audience.

Alexander Rosenblatt

Vorwort

Als ich mich entschloss, „Sleeping Beauty" zu komponieren, wusste ich, dass ich nur das Thema des sehr bekannten Walzers aus Tschaikowskys Ballett verwenden würde, ähnlich wie Paul Pabst in seiner Konzert-Paraphrase vor über 100 Jahren. Ich brachte die Melodie in ein neues Jazz-Gewand, achtete aber darauf, dass sie gleichzeitig gut erkennbar bleibt. Beim Schreiben des vierhändigen Stückes versuchte ich, klassische Jazz-Elemente (Akkorde, Rhythmen inkl. Swing, melodische Linien etc.) so natürlich und intelligent wie möglich zu integrieren, um nicht die ursprüngliche Musik zu zerstören. Ich hoffe, dass dieses Stück sehr attraktiv und wirkungsvoll für Künstler und Publikum sein wird.

Alexander Rosenblatt

Secondo

Dedicated to Serene Kato
Sleeping Beauty
Jazz Fantasy on a Theme by Tchaikovsky

Alexander Rosenblatt
* 1956

Allegro (♩ = 130–140)

Dedicated to Serene Kato

Sleeping Beauty

Jazz Fantasy on a Theme by Tchaikovsky

Alexander Rosenblatt
* 1956

Secondo

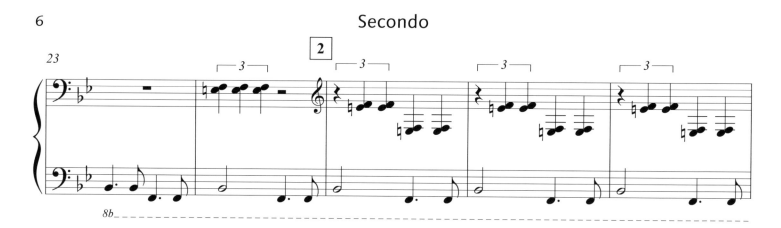

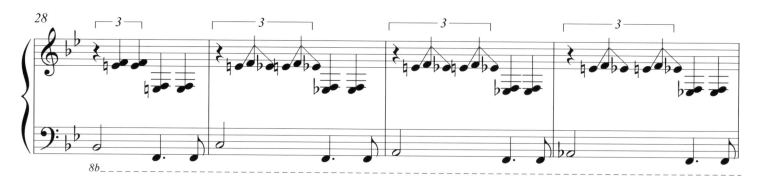

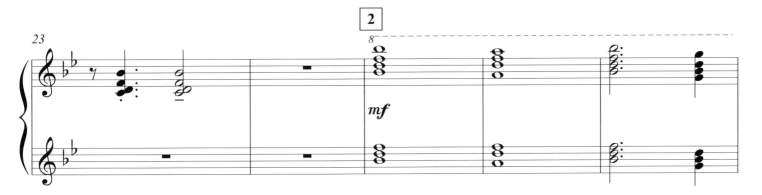

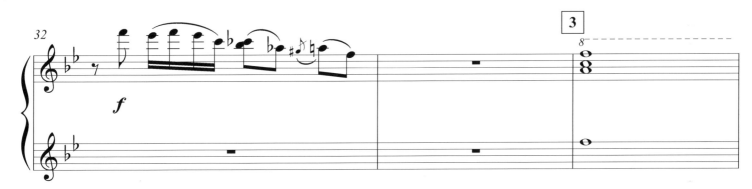

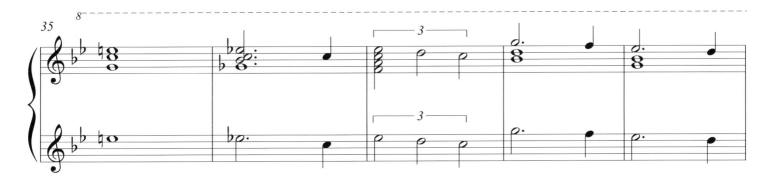

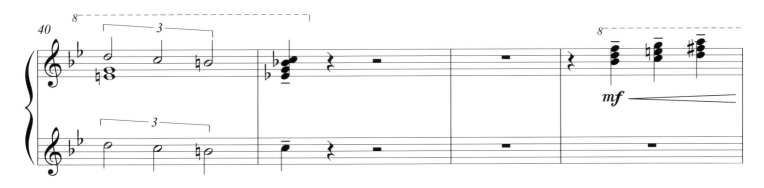

Secondo

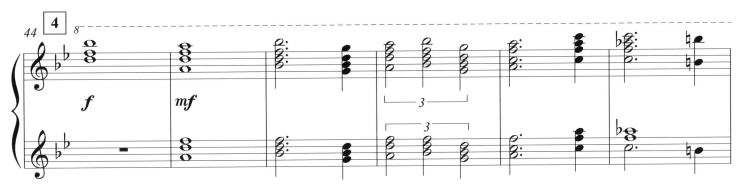

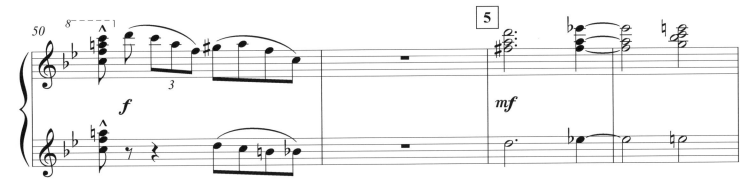

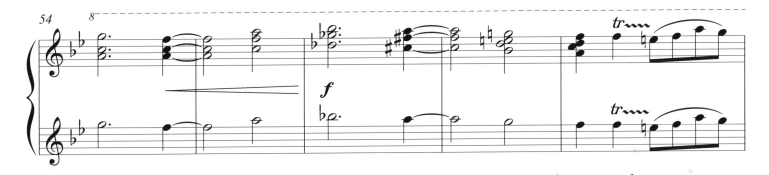

Swing (♪♪ = ♩ ♪, ♩.♪ = ♩ ♪)

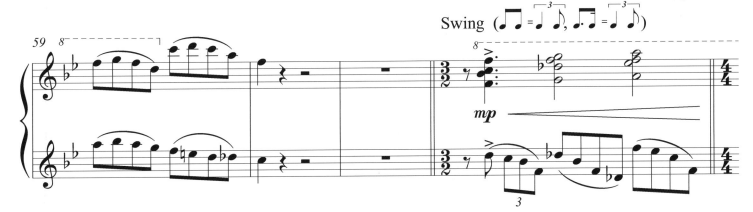

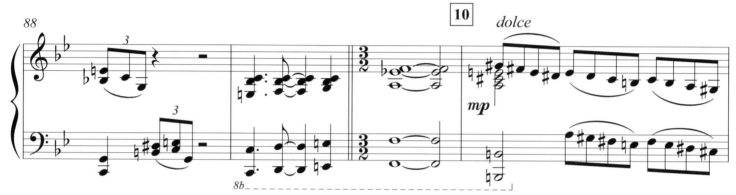

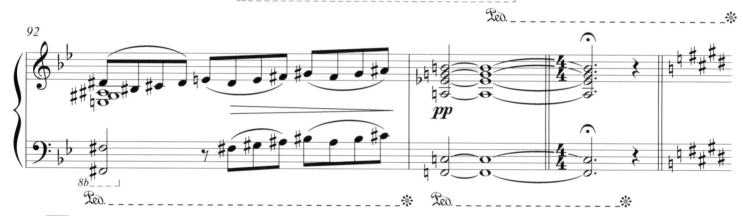

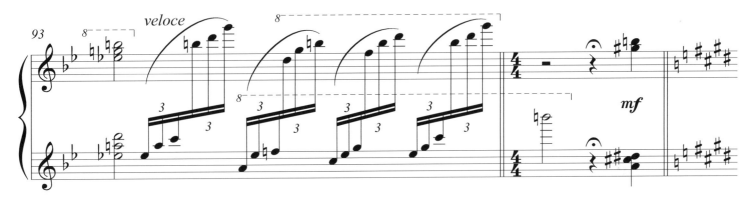

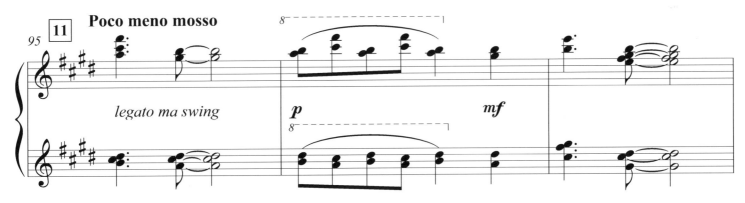

Poco meno mosso

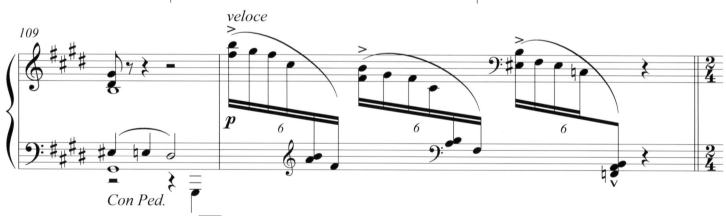

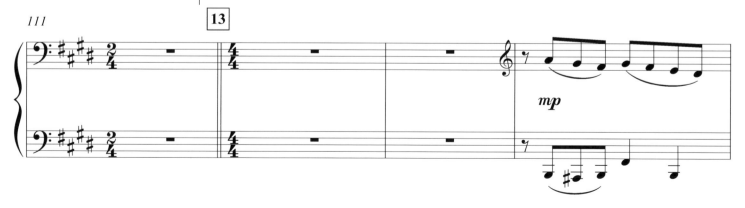

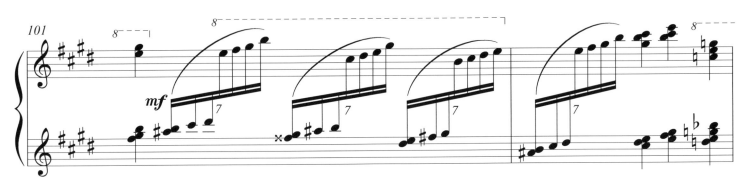

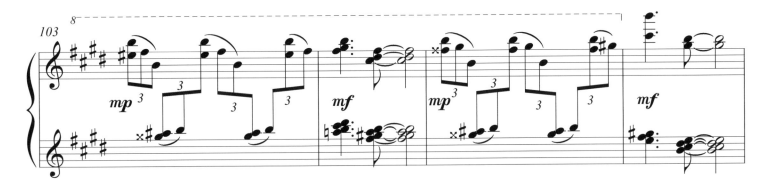

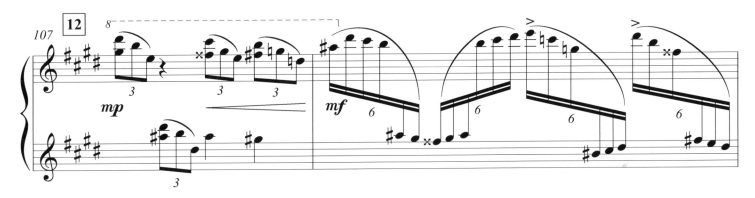

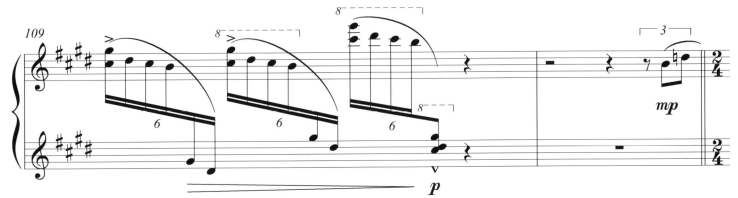

Secondo

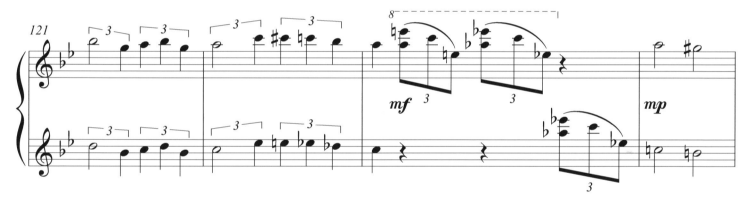

Secondo

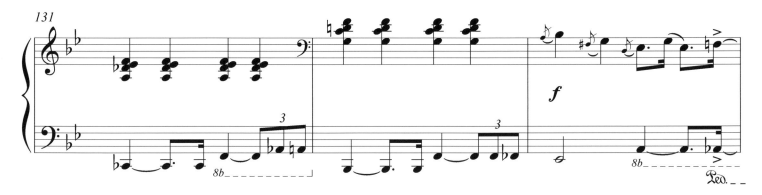

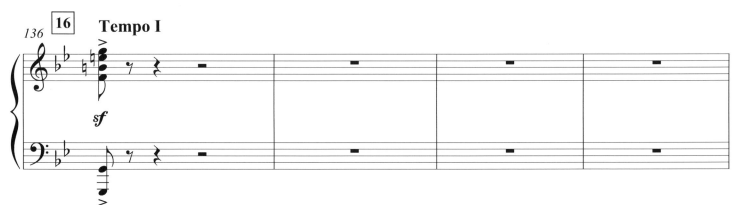

Tempo I

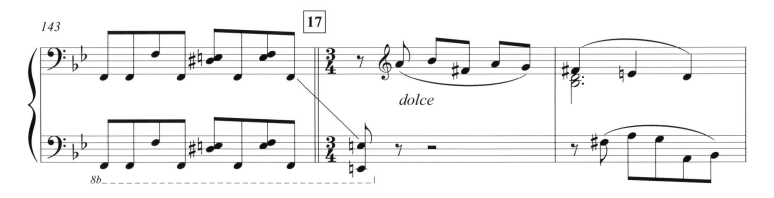

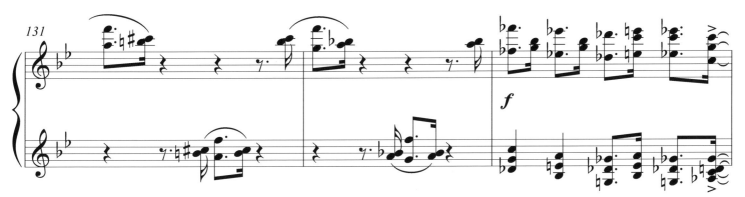

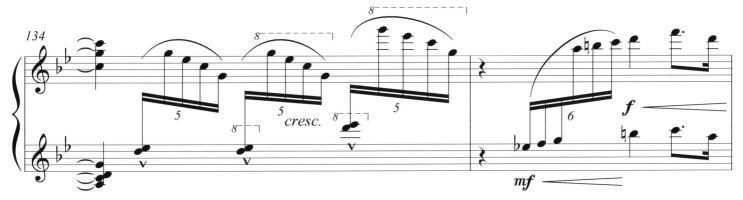

Secondo

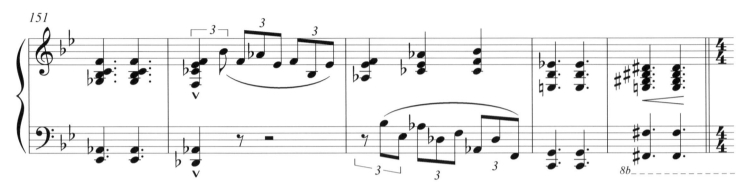

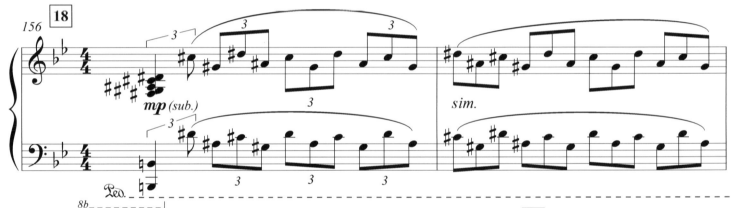

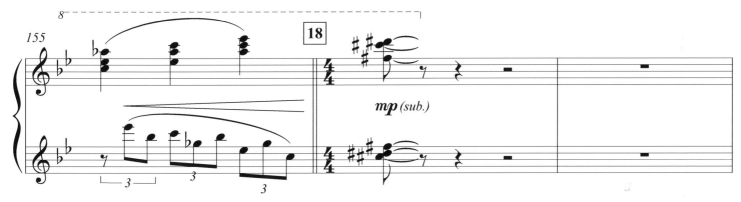

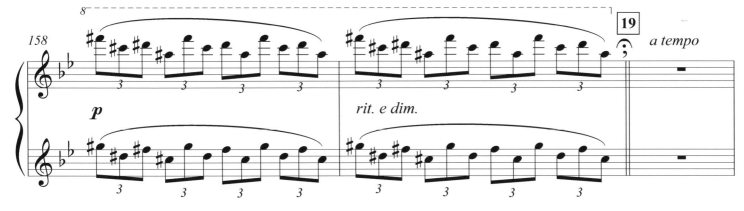
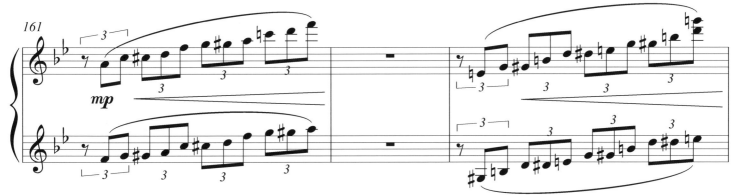

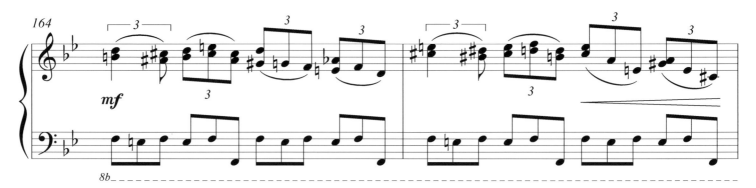

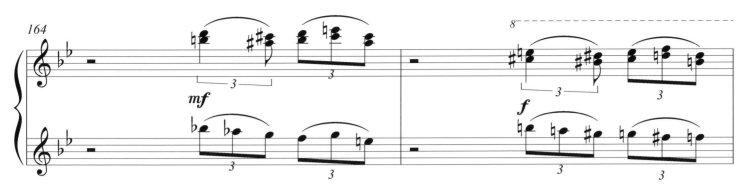

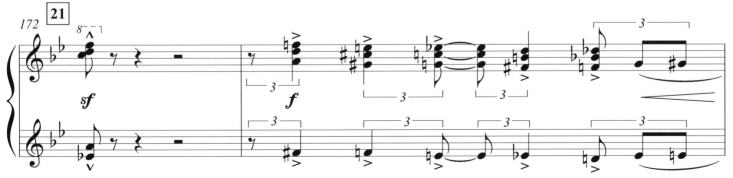

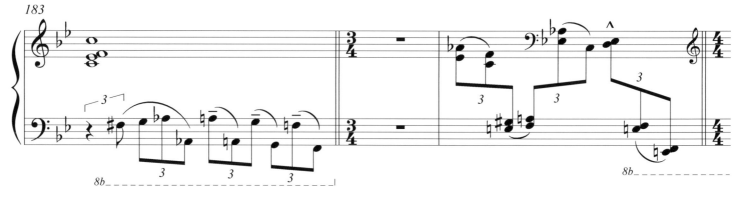

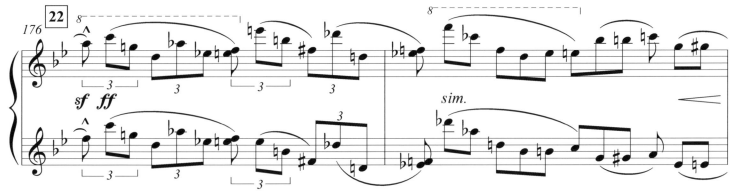

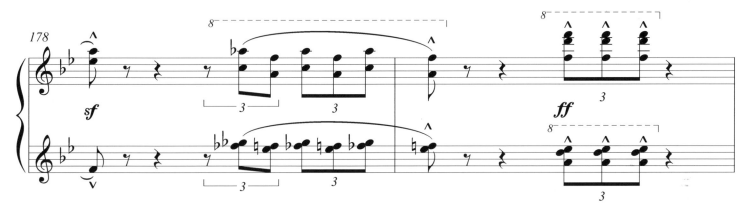

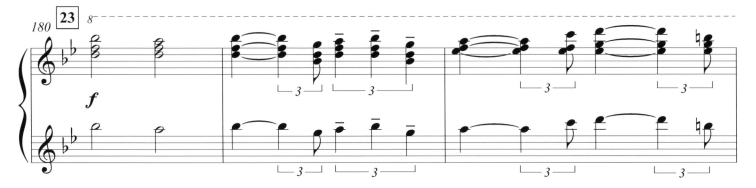

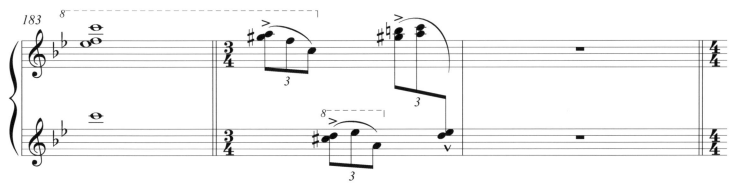

Secondo

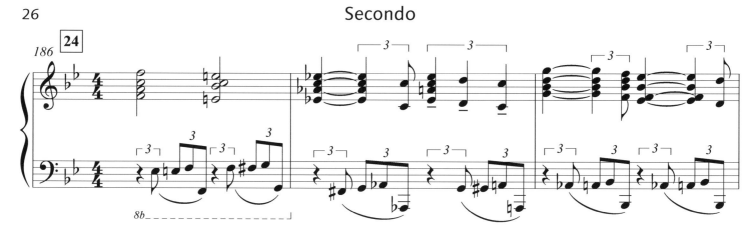

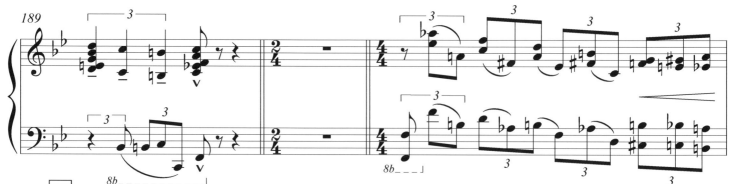

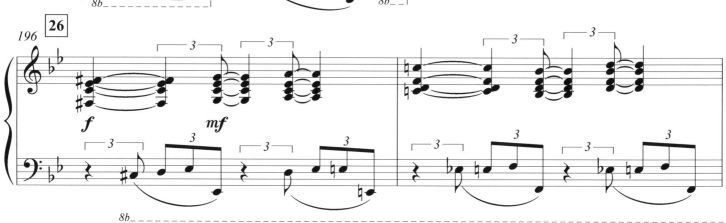

Secondo

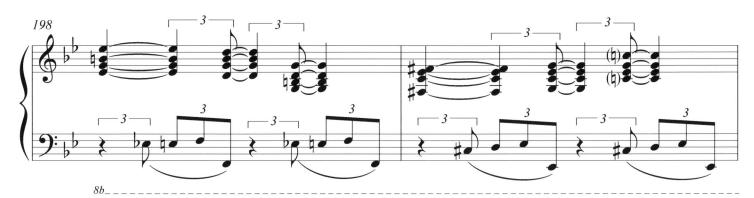

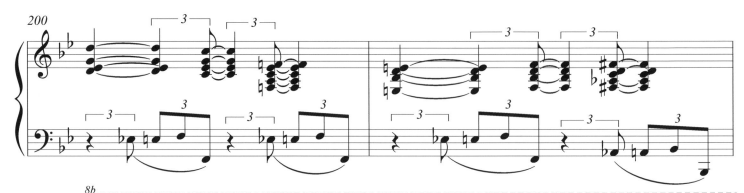

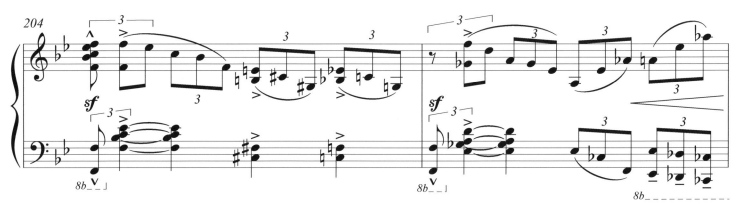

Secondo

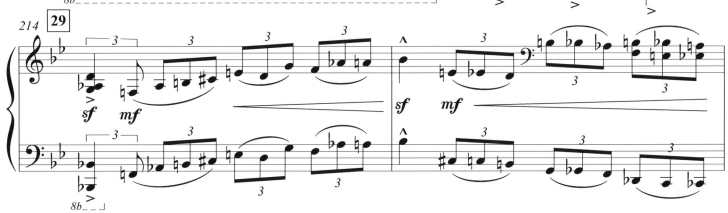

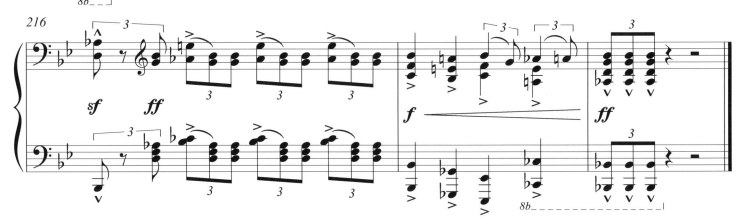